SCHOOL LIBRARY MEDIA SERIES
Edited by Diane de Cordova Biesel

1. *Chalk Talk Stories*, written and illustrated by Arden Druce, 1993.
2. *Toddler Storytime Programs*, by Diane Briggs, 1993.

D1611465

CHALK
TALK
STORIES

written and illustrated by
ARDEN DRUCE

School Library Media Series, No. 1

The Scarecrow Press, Inc.
Metuchen, N.J., & London
1993

British Library Cataloguing-in-Publication data available

Library of Congress Cataloging-in-Publication Data

Druce, Arden.
  Chalk talk stories / written and illustrated by
Arden Druce.
    p. cm. -- (School library media series ; no. 1)
  Includes bibliographical references.
  ISBN 0-8108-2781-6 (acid-free paper)
  1. Storytelling. 2. Oral interpretation.
3. Blackboard drawing. 4. Libraries, Children's--
Activity programs.   I. Title. II. Series.
  LB1042.D78 1993
  027.62'51--dc20   93-37956

Table of Contents

Editor's Foreword

The School Library Media Series is directed to the school library media specialist, particularly the building-level librarian. The multifaceted role of the librarian as educator, collection developer, curriculum developer, and information specialist is examined. The series includes concise, practical books on topical and current subjects related to programs and services.

A very special book has been chosen to launch the series. CHALK TALK STORIES, by Arden Druce, is a collection of deceptively simple original stories which can be read or told while doing line drawings on a blackboard. The stories have been carefully crafted in order to evoke a sense of wonder in youthful listeners. Each of them is reminiscent of an old folktale.

Diane de Cordova Biesel
Series Editor

Introduction

A chalk talk, the drawing of a picture on the chalk-board while telling a story, can be fun for both the student and the teacher. It not only offers opportunity for creative imagination, it also allows a brief time for relaxing.

When presenting the talks in this book, the teacher should feel free to tell the story in his or her own words, to elaborate on the text, to add more colorful words or to change the names of the people or animals.

Much of the students' enjoyment depends on having the hidden element of each story revealed gradually. Therefore, it is essential that all of the stories' titles be kept secret. Do not reveal the stories' titles.

The teacher may want to prepare the students for the fact that they are to provide the last word or words for some stories. It may be desirable to caution the class not to speak until you have signalled them to do so.

In choosing the illustrations for this book, ease of drawing and the selection of readily identifiable character-istics were uppermost in mind. If you can draw a recogniz-able picture, you can draw well enough to illustrate each story. Children's own illustrations are extremely rough. Yours, no matter how primitive, will seem good to the students. Don't hesitate to present a story because of your lack of artistic ability.

After telling a story, clarify and elaborate on any element that may be confusing. Example: In "The Little White Mouse," since the mouse you drew on the board will be larger than life, explain that you have drawn her that size so everyone can see her. Then hold out your hand and say, "Actually Little White Mouse is so small, she could fit right in my hand." Then close your hand and open it quickly and say, "Whoops, there she goes." Let your eyes follow, as if she is running away.

When preparing a story, note any words that you may need to discuss with your students after the story is told. Examples: After the story "The Little White Mouse," you may need to explain the meaning of the word "attic." If the students are unfamiliar with the word "dolphin" in the story "The Elephant," show a picture of one.

A story may lend itself to a follow-up. Example: After telling the story of "The Elephant," you may want to do the following:

1. Ask the students to tell which zoo animal is their favorite and why.
2. If appropriate for your students, have them identify pictures of zoo animals.

Any of the stories in this book can be told at any time. However, the teacher may prefer to schedule the stories for specific occasions. Examples:

Story	Occasion
The Umbrella	a rainy day

Story	Occasion
The Birthday Present	a student's birthday
The Turtle	a discussion of what to do if you're lost
The Little White Mouse	a discussion of pets
The Elephant	a discussion of zoo animals
The Frog	spring
The Halloween Witch	Halloween
Bobby Talks to Santa	Christmas
The Biggest Easter Egg	Easter
The Boat	the approach of summer
The Ice Cream Cone	a hot day
The Wagon	a discussion of saving money

Here's hoping you have as much fun telling the stories as the students will have listening to them.

THE UMBRELLA

Chan listened quietly to the sound of the rain: pitter patter, pitter patter, pitter patter. Suddenly the rain stopped, and all was still.

A big, rainbow smile spread across Chan's face. He jumped up and quickly dressed to go outside.

The hill near Chan's house was rain-soaked and very steep, but Chan began to climb it. Chan scrambled upward, digging his shoes deep into the wet ground as he went. As he rose higher, it grew harder and harder to climb with mud pulling at his feet. After a while, he stopped to rest.

1

The air was clean and fresh after the rain. Chan took
six long, deep breaths. Then, after resting a few minutes,
he got up and started to climb again.

He struggled upward through the mud, grass and rocks.
Once he fell down, but he got up and continued climbing.
On and on he went. Finally, he reached the top of the hill.

    He stood there and looked out across the valley at trees, roads and houses. How beautiful everything was. As he started down the hill, his feet slipped, and he slid a long way before he was able to stop.

"That wasn't so bad," he thought. "I think I'll slide all the way."

He balanced himself carefully, and with one great swish he slid to the bottom of the hill.

"What fun," he thought.

As he walked along, he came to a big puddle of water.
He couldn't walk around it, so he ran forward and hopped
over it.

Suddenly, he saw that there was a second puddle in front of him. It didn't look scary at all. With a quick leap, he jumped over it.

On the other side was another puddle. It was a deep puddle and very muddy.

Chan laughed and said, "Deep mud puddle, I can jump over you, too."

And with a giant leap, he soared over the puddle.

Suddenly dark clouds began to gather and, in a few minutes, raindrops began to fall. Chan laughed happily.

"Raindrops, I'm ready for you," he said. "Pitter patter all you want to."

And with that, he opened up his _____.

THE BIRTHDAY PRESENT

Nancy was very excited. It was her birthday, and since birthdays only come once a year, it was a very special day.

Her father and mother gave her a big hug and said, "Happy birthday, Nancy." Then her mother said, "Nancy, we've hidden your birthday present. You'll have to find it."

Nancy clapped her hands. "What fun," she thought.

Nancy began looking for her present. She looked all around the kitchen--by the refrigerator, under the table, on the chairs--but she didn't find a present.

O

    Then she walked through the living and family rooms.
She looked on the furniture, under the furniture, behind
the furniture.

"Since the present isn't here, maybe it's on the
porch," she thought. So she looked on the porch.

"Well, it's not on this side of the house," she said.
So she walked to the other side.

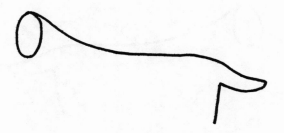

She went to her parents' room. The door was open, so she went in. She looked around, but she couldn't find a present.

Next, she walked down the hall.

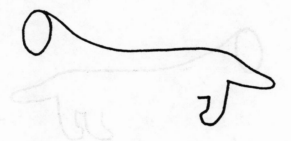

She went into her brother's room. She couldn't find
a present although she searched and searched.

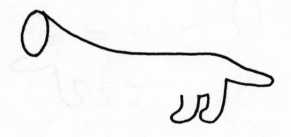

Nancy walked down the hall to her sister's room.

Inside, she looked on the bed, under the bed and in the toy box, but she couldn't find a present.

"I know," Nancy said. "It's in my room." Nancy walked
down the hall to her room.

She opened the door and went inside. Everything was
as she had left it. There was no present.

"Where can my present be? I've looked everywhere,"
Nancy thought. "Maybe it's in the yard." She rushed outside and along the fence. Suddenly Nancy's face lit up,
and she clapped her hands. There right in the middle of
the backyard was her present.

Nancy rushed over. She reached down and gave it a
big hug. "Oh," she said. "This is the best present in
the whole world."

THE TURTLE

Samantha, a small animal who lived in the woods, was very sad. She had lost her mother.

Samantha called, "Mother, mother, where are you?"

There was no answer. All was quiet.

Samantha walked along calling, "Mother, mother," but she did not find her.

⌣

When Samantha came to a hill, she climbed slowly to
the top. From there she could see the whole valley. She
saw trees, grass and a river, but she didn't see her mother.

Samantha walked to the bottom of the hill, but her mother
was not there.

She saw a little pool of water, and she circled it.

A small fish was swimming in the pool, but Samantha
didn't stop to talk.

Samantha walked along calling, "Mother, mother, where are you?"

No one answered.

Samantha came to a big bush, which she walked around.

She was very tired, so she plodded along slowly.

Next, Samantha came to a huge rock. It was too large
to climb, so Samantha made her way around it.

Samantha kept walking. She called, "Mother, mother."
Suddenly Samantha heard an answer. She turned and looked,
and there she was--there was the one she had been looking
for--there was her mother.

THE LITTLE WHITE MOUSE,
LA RATONCITA BLANCA

Jose's pet was missing. She had been missing all morning, and Jose was getting worried about her.

Jose called, "Conchita, Conchita, where are you, Little Conchita? I will look and look until I find you."

Jose looked in the living room behind the chairs, sofa and TV, but he didn't find Little Conchita.

Then he got a flashlight and climbed up into the attic. It was dark and dusty there. Jose flashed his light all around. He found a trunk and some old boxes, but he couldn't find Conchita.

"Little Conchita, where are you? I will find you,
Little Conchita."

    Jose left the attic and went downstairs. He walked
to the far end of the house.

"Where are you hiding, Conchita?"

Jose searched and searched. He walked out on the porch.

And then he walked back again.

He went to his sister's room and looked inside, but
he didn't find Conchita.

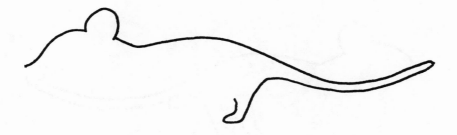

Next, Jose went to his brother's room and looked everywhere for Conchita. He looked behind the curtains, under
the bed and in the closet. He searched and searched for
Little Conchita, but he couldn't find her.

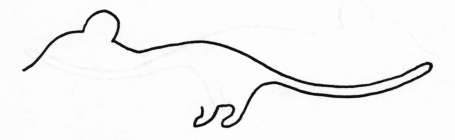

Jose walked down the hall to his parents' room. The door was open. He entered and began searching.

"Conchita, Conchita, where are you?"

Conchita did not answer.

"Maybe you are hiding in my room, Conchita."

Jose searched under his bed, behind his toy box and
all around his room, but he didn't find his pet.

Next, Jose went to the kitchen. As he looked inside, he clapped his hands in happiness. There on the table sat Conchita eating a big piece of cheese.

"Oh, little white mouse, ratoncita blanca, you are no longer lost. I have found you!"

THE ELEPHANT

It was Sunday, and many people were visiting the zoo. Susie held her father's hand as they walked about looking at the animals.

First Susie and her father looked in a pool where some playful dolphins were diving and swimming about.

Then they walked along a path where they saw some bears,
zebras and giraffes.

    Next they went into a small building where the snakes
were kept.

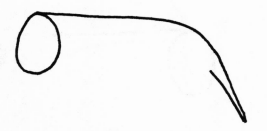

       Afterwards they continued down the path. Susie was
anxious to see her favorite wild animal, but she couldn't
seem to find it. Susie and her father walked to the aviary,
where they saw birds of all colors, kinds and sizes.

Although Susie enjoyed the birds, she looked very sad.

"Don't give up," her father said. "We'll find your
favorite wild animal."

They turned and walked a little way and found where
the monkeys were caged.

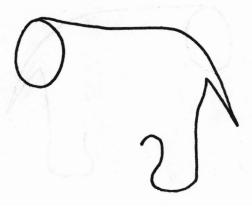

Further on they came to a food stand. They bought
some ice cream and ate it. Then they started on.

"I don't think we'll ever find my favorite animal," Susie said.

"Be patient," her father replied.

On and on they went until they came to the lions.

"We're almost to the end of the zoo," Susie said.

They walked on and on.

They came to a narrow path, which they followed. The
path turned and went back the other way. Susie and her
father continued.

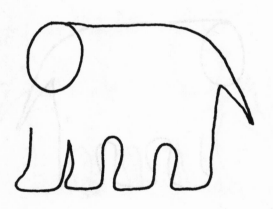

"Oh," Susie said. "I think we're getting close." She
let go of her father's hand and raced ahead.

She darted in and out among the other visitors.

Suddenly Susie called, "Oh, father, look! We've found my favorite wild animal. We've found the _____."

THE FROG

One beautiful spring day Billy went outside to enjoy the weather. He lay down on the cool grass and looked up at the sky. Suddenly he heard a strange sound.

"What was that?" he asked.

Then he heard the sound again.

"Something is here in the yard with me," he thought. "I'm not alone. Maybe whatever it is is friendly, but what if it's not?"

Billy heard the noise again. It sounded like it was over near the shed. Billy tiptoed over to look.

He didn't see anything. Just then he heard the sound
again. Maybe it was near his swing. He crept over and
looked around carefully. He didn't find anything.

Then he heard it again. This time he thought it
sounded like it was in the bushes at the side of the house.
As he approached the bushes, he picked up a stick. He used
the stick to poke around, but there was nothing to find.

The sound came louder now. Maybe whatever it was was
hiding among the flowers near the path. Billy poked among
the flowers. He saw some ants, a bug and a grasshopper,
but none of these could have made the sound.

   Was the sound coming from beneath the back steps?
Billy walked over to the steps and looked down between the
boards. All he saw were a few weeds.

The sound was now coming very often.

Billy ran over to the pond and looked into the clear, blue water.

"Oh, strange animal, come out where I can see you," Billy said.

Just then Billy saw two big eyes and a mouth in the water.

"Little green animal, with eyes so big, tell me that you are not to be feared," said Billy. "Tell me that you are my friend. Speak to me, little one. Speak to me."

"Rivet, rivet, rivet," said the _____."

THE HALLOWEEN WITCH

It was October 31st: Halloween. Gary and his sister, Betsy, had just put on their costumes. Gary was dressed as a pirate, and Betsy was dressed as a rabbit.

"Betsy, let's do something exciting today," Gary said.

"Like what?"

"Oh, I don't know," Gary replied. "Maybe like climbing Haunted Mountain."

Betsy's eyes got big and her mouth fell open. "Climbing Haunted Mountain?" she asked.

"Sure," replied Gary.

"That's too scary," said Betsy in a frightened voice.

"It's not even dark," said Gary. "We've got two more hours of daylight."

"Why do you want to climb Haunted Mountain?" asked Betsy.

"It would be fun. And besides maybe we could find out who lives there," Gary said.

"I don't think I want to know who lives there."

"Sure you do," said Gary. "Come on."

Gary and Betsy started down the street.

(Draw from right to left. ←—)

——

"Everyone has been wondering who lives on Haunted Mountain, and after today we'll be able to tell them," said Gary.

"Why don't we go by Jane's house and see if she wants to go with us?" asked Betsy.

"Okay."

They turned and walked through a vacant lot.

When they got to Jane's house, Betsy knocked on the
front door. Jane's mother answered.

"Hello, Mrs. Smith. We're on our way to Haunted
Mountain, and we wondered if Jane could go with us."

"Jane's gone to a Halloween party," Mrs. Smith replied.

"Oh," said Betsy. "Please tell her we came by. Thank
you."

Betsy and Gary cut across a lot to the main street.

Then they hurried along past one house after another.

"Let's go over to Steve's to see if he wants to go with
us," said Gary.

"All right."

They took a shortcut to Steve's house.

Gary walked up to the front door and knocked. There
was no answer. Gary knocked again. Still there was no
reply.

"I guess no one's home," said Gary.

Betsy and Gary cut back to the main street.

"Look, there's Haunted Mountain," said Betsy.

Gary and Betsy ran forward.

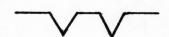

They looked up. The mountain towered high into the
sky.

"It'll be a long climb to the top," said Betsy.

"Come on," said Gary.

They began to climb.

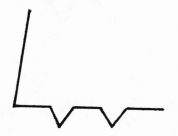

Sometimes the mountain was so steep they had to catch
hold of bushes to pull themselves up. But on they went.

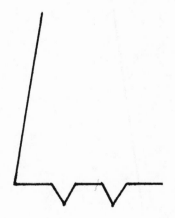

There were rocks along the way: big rocks and little
rocks. Gary and Betsy walked around the big ones and
stepped over the little ones. Higher and higher they went.

The sun shone brightly. Betsy and Gary continued
climbing. Up and up they went.

"Look," shouted Betsy. "The top of the mountain is ahead."

Betsy and Gary hurried forward.

Gary flung his arms toward the sky. "We've made it," he shouted. "We've reached the top."

"Hooray!" said Betsy.

Gary and Betsy sat down to rest. From the top of the mountain they looked out over the whole valley. In the distance, they saw trees, houses and horses.

"Gary, we've reached the top of Haunted Mountain, but we haven't found out who lives here."

"Maybe we'll find out on the way down. Or maybe who-ever it is only comes out at night," said Gary.

"Well, if whoever it is only comes out at night, I won't be here to see who it is. It's scary enough up here in the daytime. I sure wouldn't want to be here at night."

"Well, in that case, we'd better get started back," said Gary. "It's getting late."

It was very steep going down the mountain. As the
children walked, their shoes dug into the ground, often
sending small rocks rolling ahead of them.

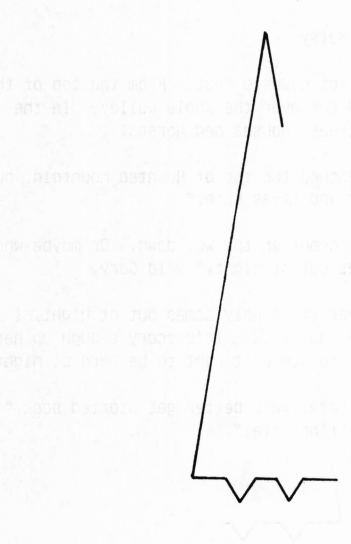

"If it weren't for the trees, we could roll down the mountain like the rocks," said Gary.

"Not in our new Halloween costumes," replied Betsy. "Come on, let's go faster."

They hurried on.

Suddenly a cloud covered the sun, and a cold breeze
swept across the mountain.

"Come on, Betsy. It's getting scary up here."

The children climbed down the mountain as fast as
they could.

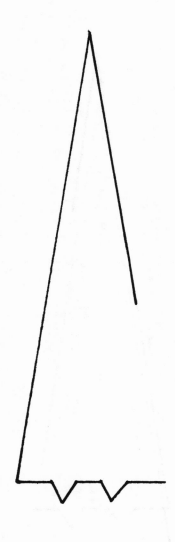

"We haven't seen anyone," said Betsy. "Maybe no one lives up here."

"People say that when the moon shines brightly on Haunted Mountain, they see a scary figure in the light."

"I'm getting scared, Gary. Let's hurry."

Down, down, down they went.

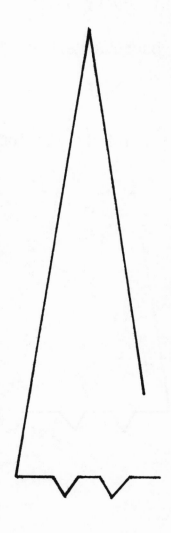

"It's almost dark. Hurry up."

"Gary, I think I heard something."

"What was it?"

"I don't know. I think it was footsteps."

"The bottom of the mountain is up ahead. Run for it."

Gary and Betsy ran quickly through the trees and down the mountain. When they reached the bottom, they sank down onto the ground, out of breath.

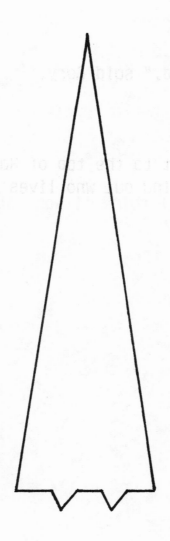

"Whew! I'm tired," said Gary.

"Me, too."

"Well, we made it to the top of Haunted Mountain and back, but we didn't find out who lives there."

Just then darkness settled across the land. Gary and Betsy turned and looked back towards the mountain. There, in a flicker of light, stood a shadowy figure with big, scary eyes.

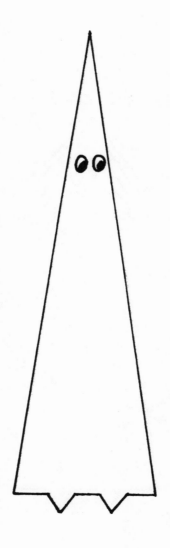

As the light began to dance over the figure, Gary and
Betsy could see long, straggly hair jutting out from both
sides of its head.

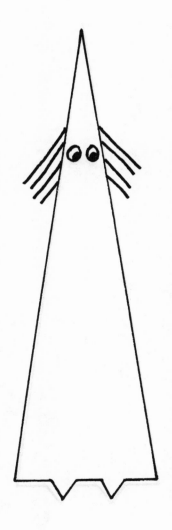

Next the moon's light swept over the figure's toothless
mouth and its huge, pointed nose.

As the moonlight flickered off and on, the children
saw that the figure was wearing a hat.

Next they noticed two arms and hands.

"Heh, heh, heh," screeched the figure.

Then it reached down and picked up a broom.

"It's going to come after us," yelled Gary. "Run!"

Gary and Betsy ran as fast as they could. When they reached their front door, they turned and looked back once more. The moon shone brightly as the scary figure screeched, "Heh, heh, heh."

"Well," said Betsy, trembling, "I guess we found out who lives on Haunted Mountain."

"It's the Halloween Witch," said Gary.

And with that, Betsy and Gary went into the house, closed the blinds and locked the doors.

BOBBY TALKS TO SANTA

Bobby was very excited; it would soon be Christmas. Today his mother was going to take him to the mall so he could talk with Santa.

When Bobby and his mother arrived at the mall, they spent several hours looking at all the beautiful things that were there. Then they went to see Santa.

Santa, who was sitting in a sleigh, looked just like Bobby thought he would. He had a long white beard, twinkly eyes and rosy cheeks. He was wearing a red cap and suit and black boots. When Santa motioned to him, Bobby climbed up onto Santa's lap. Bobby felt very good as he looked up into Santa's laughing eyes.

"My name is Bobby," he said.

"My name is Santa Claus," said Santa.

"I know," said Bobby.

"You're a fine-looking boy, Bobby."

"Thank you."

"Santa, do you know what I want for Christmas?" asked Bobby.

"Perhaps I do," said Santa. "But before we talk about that, tell me if you've been a good boy this year."

"I've been very good," said Bobby. "I've obeyed my parents and teacher, and I've tried to be good to everyone."

"Well, I'm glad to hear that," said Santa. "Have you been having a nice day here at the mall?"

"Oh, yes," said Bobby. "Mother and I have been seeing all kinds of wonderful things. First we saw the mall aviary, where there were lots of birds."

"The birds were all colors: red, blue, green, yellow.
The birds sang and sang. We walked around the aviary and
watched the birds for a long time."

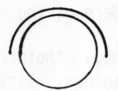

"Then we walked over to a row of shops."

"We saw dime stores, shoe stores and clothing stores."

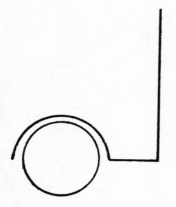

"Then we came to some furniture stores. We looked
in their windows, but we didn't go in."

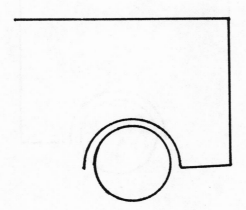

"Next, we saw some TV stores. Twenty-five TVs were
all on at the same time."

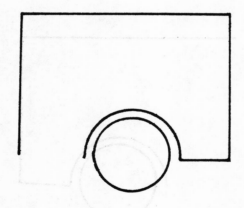

"Then we went into a book store. We saw a lot of wonderful books--books about dogs, cats, dinosaurs and lots of other things."

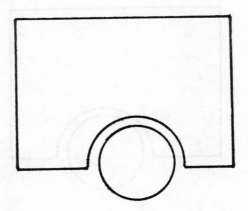

"There was a whole row of toy stores. We saw some
trains, puppets and teddy bears."

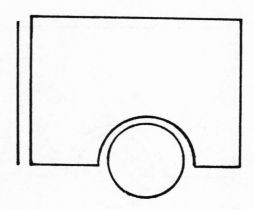

"On the corner was a flower shop. Mother bought some red flowers there."

"Then we ate lunch at a plaza. There were all kinds
of restaurants: Chinese, Mexican, Italian, American. I
ate Mexican food: tacos and enchiladas. They were really
good. Mother ate Chinese food."

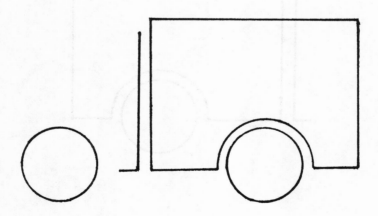

"We walked around the plaza afterwards."

"There was a candle shop on the corner. Mother bought three red candles to decorate our table for Christmas."

"At the end of the mall, we saw some candy shops."

"On the far side were some pet stores. We saw some
funny black and white puppies in one of the windows. They
were all barking at the same time."

"Then we came over here, where we found you."

"Ho! Ho! Ho! You've really had a busy day," said Santa. His eyes twinkled brightly.

Bobby said, "I wanted to see you especially so I could tell you what I want for Christmas."

"I think I know what you want," said Santa.

"You do?"

"I think so. Do you want a toy truck, Bobby?"

"How did you know?"

"Santa has ways of knowing."

Bobby reached over and hugged Santa. "I love you, Santa Claus."

"I love you, too, Bobby."

Santa set Bobby down, smiled and said, "Merry Christmas, Bobby. Merry Christmas."

THE BIGGEST EASTER EGG

(Colored chalk would be a particularly appealing medium for illustrating this story. However, white chalk will work well, too. For the best effect, draw the Easter egg as tall as the chalkboard.)

Archibald was a little rabbit. A very little rabbit. In fact, the littlest rabbit in the whole world.

Archibald loved to hop. He never walked anywhere; he always hopped. Maybe that was because he loved to hop, or maybe that was because he was a rabbit. I don't know. I never asked him.

Each year Zechariah Rabbit held an Easter egg hunt for all the bunnies in Happy Valley. According to the rules of the hunt, each bunny was supposed to find one egg and take it to Zechariah Rabbit for judging. Whoever found the biggest egg would be named Bunny of the Year. Everyone was excited. Everyone wanted to find the biggest egg.

All of the bunnies were bigger than Archibald. Some
were a little bigger. Some were a lot bigger. That didn't
bother Archibald though. He was determined to become Bunny
of the Year.

Suddenly Zechariah Rabbit blew the starting whistle,
and all the bunnies began scurrying around looking for eggs.

Archibald hopped across the meadow, looking in the tall
grass. Hop, hop, hop, hop, hop.

(Say the word "hop" every time you draw to a point.)

His little pink nose quivered as it sniffed the air.
He hopped forward eagerly. Hop, hop, hop, hop, hop.

Archibald couldn't find an egg. In the distance, he
saw Tasha Bunny hopping toward Zechariah Rabbit with a
bright red egg. He must find an egg, too. Maybe he could
find one hidden among the flowers. He looked around two
flowers, but he didn't find an egg.

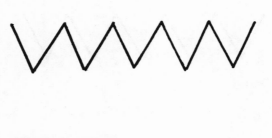

    Just then Ichabod Bunny raced past him carrying a
shiny blue egg. Surely there must be an egg hidden in the
flowers, Archibald thought. He looked around two more.

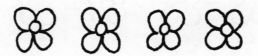

He found nothing. He looked up as Daisy Bunny whizzed
past him carrying a yellow egg. Several other bunnies with
eggs passed him, too.

Archibald began to hop about frantically looking everywhere. Hop, hop, hop, hop, hop.

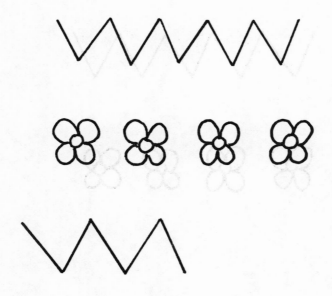

Archibald still couldn't find an egg. Three bunnies
with eggs darted past him. Archibald was about to cry, but
he kept looking. Hop, hop, hop, hop, hop.

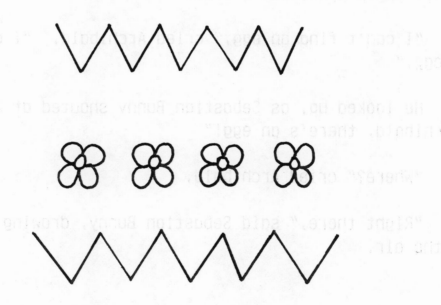

Archibald still hadn't found an egg. He looked over
at Zechariah Rabbit, where all the other bunnies had
gathered. Everyone had found an egg but him. Big tears
welled up in Archibald's eyes.

"I can't find an egg," cried Archibald. "I can't find
an egg."

He looked up, as Sebastian Bunny shouted at him.
"Archibald, there's an egg!"

"Where?" cried Archibald.

"Right there," said Sebastian Bunny, drawing a circle
in the air.

Archibald began running around in a circle.

When he looked up, he saw an egg. A big egg, a very
big egg. An enormous egg. Archibald happily rolled the
egg over to where Zechariah Rabbit and the other bunnies
stood waiting.

Zechariah looked at all of the eggs that had been
found. They were all colors: red, blue, green, yellow,
orange, purple, black. They were all sizes: tiny, little,
big, bigger, biggest.

All the rabbits hopped about restlessly looking at
eggs, counting them, comparing them. Suddenly Zechariah
Rabbit blew his whistle. Everyone stood still, waiting
breathlessly for the winner of the Easter egg hunt to be
announced.

Zechariah Rabbit's voice boomed forth. "The biggest egg of all was found by the littlest bunny. I hereby proclaim little Archibald as Bunny of the Year!"

Archibald leaped high into the air. He had won! Hooray! He had won!

Archibald gave a hug to his friend Sebastian, and the two leaped about happily.

The other bunnies leaped into the air, too. "Hooray for Archibald," they shouted. "Hooray for the Bunny of the Year!"

THE BOAT

Jimmy raced along the beach.

Warm sand squished between his toes as he ran.

He climbed up onto a big rock and looked out across
the ocean.

The water looked cool and inviting. He jumped in.
He swam and swam.

When he got tired, he swam back to the beach.

    While he lay resting in the warm sand, he noticed a
flag flying far in the distance.

"I think I can swim out to that flag," he thought.

He ran and jumped into the water and began swimming. He swam and swam until he reached the flag.

Suddenly the ocean got very rough. Jimmy lay still
and let the water pick him up and carry him toward shore.

"What fun," he thought.

He swam and swam.

Jimmy was getting tired, so tired he could hardly swim.
He knew he didn't have the strength to swim back to shore.

"I think I can swim a little further," he thought.

With all his energy he swam forward.

   The shore was a long way off. There was no way he
could swim that far. He was so tired he was about to give
up, about to let himself be swallowed by the ocean. Suddenly when he thought he would drown, when he thought all
was lost, things changed. Suddenly he looked up, and he
knew he was going to be rescued.

    He knew it with his heart, he knew it with his mind.
And he knew it with his eyes, because there right before
him was a _____.

THE ICE CREAM CONE

It was a beautiful day. The sun was shining, the air
was clean and birds were singing. Angie strapped on her
roller skates and skated down the sidewalk.

At the corner, she stopped. As she waited for the
signal to change to green, something lying in the gutter
caught her eye. It was bright and shiny. She reached
down and picked it up. It was a silver coin--a fifty-cent
piece.

"Wow," she thought. She couldn't ask if anyone had
lost it, because no one was around. She put the coin in
her pocket. Then she turned and skated in the opposite
direction.

When she got to the top of the hill, she skated to the
left.

"I know what I want to buy with my fifty cents," Angie
thought happily to herself.

Angie was a good skater. She spun around on her skates.

Then she made another fancy circle.

She whirled around again.

Then she skated into a store, put her fifty cents on the counter and bought a three-scoop-vanilla-chocolate-strawberry _____ _____ _____.

THE WAGON

Danny was saving his money. There was something he
wanted very much.

One day, Danny helped his father wash the car. It
took a long time. The car was very dirty. After Danny
hosed the car off, his father drove it into the garage.
Then Danny hosed the driveway off.

(Draw from left to right. ⟶)

_____

Danny's father said, "Danny, you always do a good job helping." Then he added, "Your mother and I know there's something you want very badly. We've decided to let you earn the money to buy it. Every time you help around the house or yard, we'll give you some money until you've earned what you need."

Danny ran and hugged his father. Lucky, Danny's dog, knew something exciting was happening. He ran over and licked Danny's face with a big slobbery kiss.

The next day when Grandfather came over, Danny helped
him rake leaves in the front yard. There were lots of
leaves: red, brown and yellow ones. Danny raked them up
into piles and then scooped them into bags.

Grandfather was very pleased with Danny's work. He
gave him several bright, shiny coins.

On Tuesday, Mr. Williams, Danny's neighbor, asked
Danny if he'd take his dog, Max, for a walk. Danny said
he'd like to. Danny walked Max all the way down Maple
Street. It was a long walk. Danny and Max walked past
the library, the school and the grocery store.

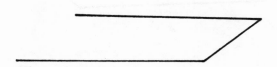

When they got back home, Mr. Williams gave Danny
twenty-five cents. Danny dropped the money into his piggy
bank.

One day, Danny helped his mother dry dishes. When he
finished, he lined all the dishes up near the cupboard so
Mother could put them away.

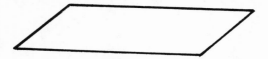

Mother said Danny had done a good job. She hugged him
and gave him a quarter.

Every day Danny's piggy bank was getting fuller and
fuller.

On Thursday, Danny noticed that the wastebasket in the
kitchen was very full. He picked it up, carried it outside
and emptied it into a trash can. Then he went about the
house gathering up all the wastebaskets and emptying them.

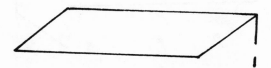

That night he was pleased to find a dime on his pillow.

Another day Danny weeded some flowers that were grow-
ing along the side of the house. He liked weeding. It was
fun digging into the rich, brown soil and loosening weeds.

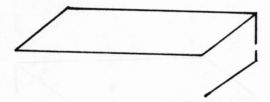

When Danny's mother saw the work he had done, she said,
"Danny, what a good job you did." Then she went into Danny's bedroom and dropped a coin into his bank.

When Mr. Williams had to go away for the day, he asked
Danny if he'd feed and water his dog, Max, and his cat,
Fluffy. Danny said he'd be glad to. When it was feeding
time, Danny put out fresh water for Max and Fluffy and
filled their food bowls.

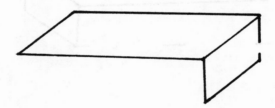

When Mr. Williams got back, he gave a quarter to Danny.

One day there was a dust storm. The wind blew and
blew. It blew dust in through all the living-room windows.
Danny got a dust cloth and wiped all the dust up.

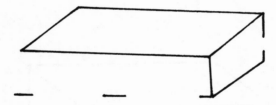

Grandmother, who was visiting, kissed Danny and said,
"You're such a good boy. You didn't even have to be asked
to do what needed to be done." Then she handed two shiny
coins to Danny. "Put those in your piggy bank," she said.

    On Saturday, Danny found some cans and bottles in the
alley. After getting permission from his mother, he hurried
to the store with them. Lucky raced along with him, barking
happily.

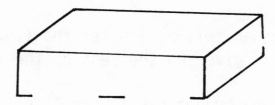

    Mr. Brown, the grocer, gave Danny fifteen cents for the
cans and bottles.

    Danny's bank was almost full now.

Finally one day, Danny took all the money out of his bank, and he and his father counted it. "You only need fifty cents more," his father said.

Danny had been working very hard. He had been saving for weeks. He didn't know where he would get fifty cents more.

Danny's father smiled. "Water the flower and vegetable gardens, and I'll give you the rest of the money you need."

Danny ran and hugged his father. Then he rushed out into the yard, got the hose and watered the flower garden.

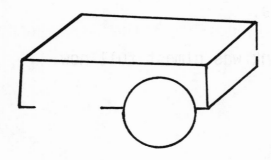

Then he watered the vegetable garden.

When he finished, his father gave Danny fifty cents.

    That afternoon, Danny and his father took all the money
out of the piggy bank and put it into a bag.

    Father said, "You've worked very hard, Danny. You've
saved your money carefully, and now you have enough to buy
what you want. You may go to the store, if you'd like to."

    Danny was so happy. He thanked his father, picked up
the bag of money and started off.

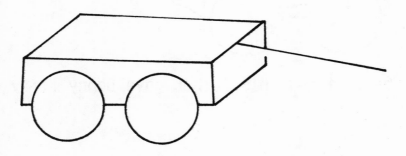

When Danny got to the store, he turned and saw that Lucky was running down the street after him.

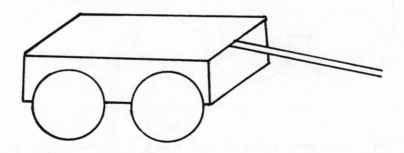

When Lucky caught up, Danny told him to sit outside
the store and wait.   Then Danny went inside.

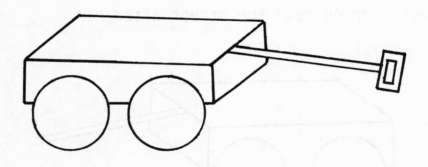

      This was the day Danny had been working and saving for--
the day he had been looking forward to for so long.   TODAY
HE WOULD BUY SOMETHING HE WANTED VERY MUCH.   Today he would
buy a _____.

Bibliography

Pflomm, Phyllis Noe. CHALK IN HAND: THE DRAW AND TELL BOOK.
New Jersey: Scarecrow Press, 1986.

A collection of chalk talk stories, poems and theme setters
for pre-school through grade 3.

Withers, Carl. THE TALE OF A BLACK CAT. New York: Holt,
Rinehart and Winston, 1966.

A well-known chalk talk story. Now out of print, but may
be obtainable through interlibrary loan.

About the Author

Arden Druce has been a school librarian for twenty-one years, serving elementary, junior and senior high schools. She has also been a teacher of grades one through six.

Mrs. Druce received an MLS from the University of Southern California and a BA in Education from Los Angeles State College.

She is the author of COMPLETE LIBRARY SKILLS ACTIVITIES PROGRAM (originally titled LIBRARY SKILLS: LESSONS FOR GRADES k-6); LIBRARY LESSONS FOR GRADES 7-9; and an interactive picture book, WITCH, WITCH.

Now retired, she lives in Camp Verde, Arizona.